Study Guide

Glencoe

RESPONSIBLE DRIVING

drivered.glencoe.com

Heathrow, Florida

Mc Graw Hill **Glencoe**

New York, New York   Columbus, Ohio   Chicago, Illinois

Glencoe

The **McGraw·Hill** Companies

Send all inquiries to:

Glencoe/McGraw-Hill
4400 Easton Commons
Columbus, OH 43219

ISBN 0-07-873048-1 (Responsible Driving Study Guide Student Edition)
ISBN 0-07-873049-X (Responsible Driving Study Guide Teacher Annotated Edition)

Printed in the United States of America.

10 11 12 13   HES 16 15 14 13

TABLE OF CONTENTS

TABLE OF CONTENTS

TABLE OF CONTENTS

CHAPTER 1 Driving and Mobility

STUDY GUIDE FOR CHAPTER 1   LESSON 1

Mobility and Driver Education

A. Driver education courses have many great benefits. What do you think the results would be in the long run, say in 20 years, on the following rates and statistics if there were no driver education courses?

1. Insurance rates _____

_____

2. Accident rates _____

_____

3. Drinking and driving conviction rates _____

_____

4. Traffic deaths _____

_____

B. Describe briefly your personality as you think it will affect your driving. What is your maturity level? Do you get upset easily? What kinds of situations annoy you?

_____

_____

_____

_____

C. FIND OUT MORE. Call a local vehicle insurance company and ask if you can take a few minutes to ask some questions. Ask what the insurance rates will be for you when you are ready to drive. Also, ask what the rates would be for someone your age who is not taking any driver education classes. What will the rates be when you are 25 years old? What are they for a person without driver education? What are they for someone convicted of driving while intoxicated?

_____

_____

_____

_____

_____

The Highway Transportation System

A.   The National Highway Safety Act controls the regulations for vehicle registration, road construction and maintenance, and driver licensing. What do you think the effects on the following would be if suddenly we had no National Highway Safety Act?

Roads and Highways: _____

_____

Drivers and Pedestrians: _____

_____

Cars and Trucks: _____

_____

B.   Although each state has its own laws governing the use of motor vehicles, the federal government has also set national highway and driving standards. Tell by marking S or F next to the provision whether it is a state or a federal law.

_____   **1.**   Establishes the maximum speed that may be driven anywhere.

_____   **2.**   Sets national standards for all motor vehicle equipment.

_____   **3.**   Regulates vehicle inspection.

_____   **4.**   Enforces traffic laws.

_____   **5.**   Tells what highway maintenance the state must provide.

_____   **6.**   Regulates vehicle registration.

_____   **7.**   Instructs automobile manufacturers about what safety devices they must provide.

_____   **8.**   Assigns points to driver's record for traffic violations.

_____   **9.**   Regulates driver licensing.

_____   **10.**   Requires the vehicle manufacturer to recall a vehicle and correct any defects discovered after a vehicle is sold.

C.   FIND OUT MORE. Interview somebody you know who is a driver. Ask that person what he or she does personally to reduce risk when driving. What does the driver do to keep the vehicle in good, safe condition? What does she or he do to anticipate the actions of others? Do the driver and all passengers wear seat belts? Has the driver ever driven while very tired or sick? What has the driver done in the last year to improve his or her driving skills? Write your findings on a separate piece of paper.

STUDY GUIDE FOR CHAPTER 1   LESSON 3

The Risks of Driving

A. For each sentence below, circle T if the statement is true and F if it is false. Correct each false statement in the space provided below.

   1. Driving does not involve risk.   T   F

   _____

   2. In any given year, the likelihood of your being involved in a crash is about 1 in 9.   T   F

   _____

   3. Driving involves risk even for experienced drivers.   T   F

   _____

   4. When you are driving, increasing your visibility also increases risk.   T   F

   _____

   5. The foundations of effective driving include searching and giving meaning, understanding options and choices, and mastering basic driving skills.   T   F

   _____

B. In the space below, name the five steps you can take to reduce risk while driving.

   _____

   _____

   _____

   _____

   _____

C. FIND OUT MORE. Risk rates are affected by such factors as population. Research collision statistics for your state and city. Report your findings below, and suggest ways in which risk could be reduced.

   _____

   _____

   _____

   _____

   _____

STUDY GUIDE FOR CHAPTER 1   LESSON 4

The Costs of Driving

A. Complete the sentences below by filling in the blanks with the correct words.

1. The costs of driving can be divided into crash costs and _____ costs.

2. Crash costs are measured in dollars and in _____.

3. Fixing wrecked vehicles, repairing property damage, and caring for the injured contribute to _____ costs.

4. A seat belt is an example of a _____ that can help prevent crash costs.

5. Driving while under _____ causes 13,000 fatalities, 360,000 nonfatal injuries, and nearly $40 billion a year in crash costs.

6. Driving at an _____ speed reduces crash costs.

7. Three preventable mistakes linked to high numbers of crashes are _____ , _____ , and _____ .

8. The noncrash costs of driving include _____ costs, _____ costs, and _____ costs.

9. Gas, oil, and tires contribute to the _____ costs that maintain your motor vehicle.

10. The _____ miles you drive, the greater are your operating costs.

11. The more miles you drive, the _____ are your fixed costs.

B. FIND OUT MORE. Go to your local library and research recent efforts to regulate and to reduce motor-vehicle-related pollution. How have such regulations affected the environmental costs of driving in your state? How have environmental costs affected your personal cost-benefit ratio of driving?

_____

_____

_____

_____

_____

_____

_____

_____

CHAPTER 2   Administrative and Traffic Laws

STUDY GUIDE FOR CHAPTER 2   LESSON 1

Administrative Laws

A. For each sentence below, circle T if the statement is true and F if it is false. If a statement is false, correct it in the space provided below.

1. Administrative laws apply only to traffic violations.   T   F

_____

2. A point system enables the state to keep track of a driver's violations.   T   F

_____

3. A certificate of title is the same as a certificate of registration.   T   F

_____

4. Driving tests are designed and administered by the federal government.   T   F

_____

5. You receive your license plates when you receive your certificate of title.   T   F

_____

6. For your driver's license, you will be tested on traffic laws and knowledge of signs, car repair, and signals.   T   F

_____

7. A driver's license that is suspended is usually taken away for a period of 10 to 15 days.   T   F

_____

B. FIND OUT MORE. Look in your state driver's manual and see whether your state uses a point system. If so, how many points does it take to lose your license? How many points are given for speeding at 15 miles per hour over the speed limit? If your state does not use a point system, what does the driver's manual say about guidelines the state uses to take away a driver's license?

_____

_____

_____

_____

_____

_____

Right-of-Way Rules

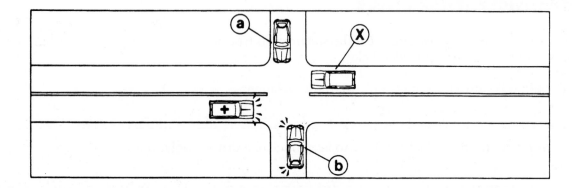

A. You are driving vehicle X. Who must yield the right-of-way? _____

Why? _____

_____

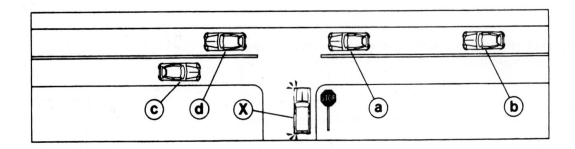

B. You are driving vehicle X. Which vehicles may go through the intersection first?

_____

Last? _____

Why? _____

C. FIND OUT MORE. Go to a four-way stop in your area and bring a pencil and pad of paper. Count the total number of vehicles that pass through the intersection in 30 minutes. How many drivers proceeded through the four-way stop correctly? What percentage went through incorrectly?

_____

_____

STUDY GUIDE FOR CHAPTER 2   LESSON 3

Speed Limits

A. Explain the basic speed law, and give an example of how it works.

_____

_____

_____

_____

_____

_____

_____

_____

B. FIND OUT MORE. Using your state driver's manual, answer the following questions.

1. What is the maximum speed limit on the interstates in your state?

_____

2. Does your state have a night speed limit on your interstate highways that is different from the day speed limit?

_____

3. Does your state have a different speed limit for trucks than for other vehicles?

_____

4. What, if any, is the minimum speed limit on your interstate highways?

_____

5. What is the speed limit on state roads where the speed is not posted?

_____

6. What is the speed limit for school zones in your state?

_____

7. What is the speed limit in business or recreation areas in your state?

_____

Driver-Condition Laws

A. For each sentence below, circle T if the statement is true and F if it is false. Correct each false statement in the space provided below.

1. Your physical, mental, and emotional conditions affect your ability to drive safely.   T   F

_____

2. As a licensed driver, you do not have to take a blood alcohol concentration (BAC) test if a police officer asks you to.   T   F

_____

3. In many states, drivers who test above the blood alcohol concentration limit can have their licenses suspended for 7 to 180 days for a first offense.   T   F

_____

4. Speeding, tailgating, and running red lights are examples of aggressive driving.   T   F

_____

B. Road rage is defined as a driver's uncontrolled anger that is expressed in aggressive or violent behavior behind the wheel. In the space provided below, list four ways to minimize risk when dealing with a driver who is experiencing road rage.

_____

_____

_____

_____

C. FIND OUT MORE. Research your state's specific blood alcohol concentration limit. What penalties can a driver face if he or she operates a motor vehicle while above the BAC limit?

_____

_____

_____

_____

_____

CHAPTER 3 Signs, Signals, and Pavement Markings

STUDY GUIDE FOR CHAPTER 3   LESSON 1

Regulatory and Warning Signs

A. Look at the shapes of the signs below. Under each sign, explain what kind of sign it is and what it means.

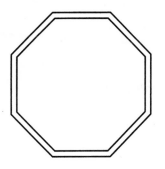

1. _____

_____

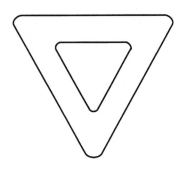

2. _____

_____

3. _____

_____

4. _____

_____

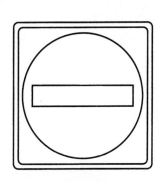

5. _____

_____

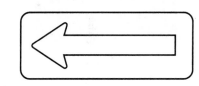

6. _____

_____

B. FIND OUT MORE. In the next week, take notes on your way to and from school. What regulatory and warning signs are there on this route?

_____

_____

_____

_____

_____

Guide and International Signs

A. Write the letter of the statement that defines each sign below.

A = Route Marker   **B** = Destination Sign   **C** = International Sign
D = Recreational Area Sign   **E** = Roadside Services

1. _____

_____

2. _____

_____

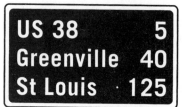

3. _____

_____

4. _____

_____

5. _____

_____

6. _____

_____

7. _____

_____

8. _____

_____

9. _____

_____

B. In the next week, look over the roads in your area. What international signs, if any, exist where you live? Where are they located?

_____

Pavement Markings

A. Select the phrase that best completes each sentence below. Write the letter of the answer you have chosen to the left of each question.

_____ **1.** Yellow lines separate traffic going

a. in opposite directions.

b. in the same direction.

c. off an exit ramp.

d. around a curve.

_____ **2.** A solid yellow line to your left on the road means that you are in or at

a. a railroad crossing.

b. a no-passing zone.

c. a one-way street.

d. an intersection.

_____ **3.** White lines parallel to the roadway

a. separate traffic going in opposite directions.

b. separate traffic going in the same direction.

c. separate parking spaces.

d. separate traffic around curves.

_____ **4.** On divided highways, a single solid yellow line

a. marks the right edge of the roadway.

b. means that you may not pass.

c. marks the left edge of the roadway.

d. means none of the above.

B. In the space below, three passing situations are described. In the space above the descriptions, draw in the roadway markings that would show the passing situation. With arrows, indicate the direction in which your vehicle is moving.

Do not pass in either direction.   Pass only in your direction.   Legal only for oncoming vehicles to pass.

C. FIND OUT MORE. In the next week, see if you can find an example of an area that has diagonal "zebra" lines on the pavement. Where did you find this marking? What do the lines mean?

_____

_____

Traffic-Control Devices

A. Look at the following lane-use lights. Describe what they mean in the space below.

| 1. Red X | 2. Green arrow | 3. Yellow X | 4. Flashing yellow X |

Red X _____

Green arrow _____

Yellow X _____

Flashing yellow X _____

B. Describe the actions that you should take if you encounter the following traffic signals.

1. At a flashing signal, you should either _____ or _____.

2. A flashing red signal means _____.

3. At a flashing yellow signal, you should _____.

4. If a police officer is directing traffic at a signal, you should _____.

C. FIND OUT MORE. Call your state's department of motor vehicles and ask them what the procedure is for a physically challenged person to get a driver's license in your state. How are the tests administered? For what length of time are the licenses issued?

_____

_____

_____

_____

CHAPTER 4 Systems and Checks Prior to Driving

STUDY GUIDE FOR CHAPTER 4   LESSON 1

Comfort and Control Systems

A. Match the vehicle part on the left with a description of one of the part's functions on the right.

_____	**1.** air conditioner	**a.** turns on the vehicles electrical system
_____	**2.** air vents	**b.** makes your vehicle stop without a lot of foot power
_____	**3.** ignition switch	**c.** maintains speed so that you do not have to use the accelerator
_____	**4.** accelerator pedal	**d.** lowers the vehicle's humidity
_____	**5.** parking brake	**e.** controls the direction in which the vehicle is going
_____	**6.** power brakes	**f.** keeps a stopped vehicle from rolling
_____	**7.** cruise control	**g.** allows outside air to flow into the vehicle
_____	**8.** steering wheel	**h.** controls speed
_____	**9.** brake pedal	**i.** allows you to switch gears with a manual transmission
_____	**10.** clutch pedal	**j.** enables you to slow or stop your vehicle

B. The ignition system has five positions. What are they, and what do they do?

1. _____

2. _____

3. _____

4. _____

5. _____

C. FIND OUT MORE. Talk with somebody you know who has a vehicle with cruise control. Find out when this person uses cruise control. Does the person feel that less concentration is needed on the road because of cruise control?

_____

_____

_____

_____

_____

Visibility and Protective Systems

A. For each sentence below, circle T if the statement is true and F if it is false. Correct each false statement in the space below.

1. Your side-marker lights come on when you turn on your headlights.   T   F

_____

2. A good set of mirrors will eliminate all blind spots.   T   F

_____

3. You can rely exclusively on your mirrors when backing up.   T   F

_____

4. If you are wearing a shoulder-lap seat belt at the time of a crash, your risk of being killed is reduced by 50 percent.   T   F

_____

5. An example of a passive safety device is an air bag.   T   F

_____

6. All states require very young children to ride in safety-tested and approved car seats.   T   F

_____

7. Air bags are most effective in preventing injuries in rear-end crashes.   T   F

_____

8. Head restraints are valuable in preventing injuries to the head because the restraints prevent your head from hitting the steering wheel.   T   F

_____

B. FIND OUT MORE. Ask an adult to move a vehicle to an open area. Get into the driver's seat, and adjust the mirrors so that you can see as much of what is behind and next to you as possible. Have someone else in the class walk around the vehicle while you observe the person. Where are the blind spots in that vehicle? Draw a diagram below.

STUDY GUIDE FOR CHAPTER 4   LESSON 3

Information and Communication Systems

A. For each sentence below, circle T if the statement is true and F if it is false. Correct each false statement in the space below.

1. If your alternator warning light comes on, you should turn off any unnecessary electrical devices and check with a mechanic as soon as possible.   T   F

   _____

2. The oil-pressure gauge tells you if your vehicle is low on oil.   T   F

   _____

3. If brake fluid is leaking, the brake warning light will come on.   T   F

   _____

4. Your vehicle's backup lights are red or amber and come on when you shift into Reverse.   T   F

   _____

5. Vehicles are required by law to have a license-plate light.   T   F

   _____

B. What does each of the following do?

1. Speedometer _____

2. Fuel gauge _____

3. High-beam indicator _____

4. Temperature gauge _____

5. Alternator _____

6. Oil pressure gauge _____

7. Emergency flashers _____

8. Odometer _____

C. FIND OUT MORE. Ask someone you know who drives what the effect would be on the vehicle's safety if each of the above did not work. Summarize the responses below.

   _____

   _____

   _____

Checking Your Vehicle Before Driving

A. For each sentence below, circle T if the statement is true and F if it is false. Correct each false statement in the space below.

1. Each year, about 200 children under the age of six are killed while playing in the family driveway.   T   F

   _____

2. You should inspect the area around your vehicle after you get into it.   T   F

   _____

3. You should check the level of engine oil once a month.   T   F

   _____

4. When checking the battery, you should check for corrosion.   T   F

   _____

5. You should always load packages from the roadside of a parked vehicle.   T   F

   _____

6. When entering a vehicle, you should walk around the front of the vehicle, facing traffic.   T   F

   _____

B. What procedures should you follow for an inside-the-vehicle check before you start the vehicle?

_____

_____

_____

_____

_____

C. FIND OUT MORE. For the next two weeks, keep a record of every time you ride in a vehicle as a passenger. How many times did the driver check to see that you were wearing a seat belt?

_____

_____

_____

_____

CHAPTER 5 | Basic Control Tasks

STUDY GUIDE FOR CHAPTER 5   LESSON 1

Using an Automatic Transmission

A. The following sentences are procedures for starting a car with an automatic transmission. However, they are in the wrong order. Write the number that identifies the correct order of each step in the space to the left.

_____ **a.** Turn the ignition key to the Start position. Release as soon as the engine starts.

_____ **b.** If you do not have an automatic fuel-injection system, set the automatic choke by pressing the accelerator pedal once to the floor and releasing it.

_____ **c.** Make sure that the gear selector lever is in Park.

_____ **d.** Press the accelerator lightly with your foot and hold it.

_____ **e.** As the engine idles, check your gauges to be sure that the oil-pressure system and other systems are working.

_____ **f.** Make sure that the parking brake is set.

B. For each sentence below, circle T if the statement is true and F if it is false. Correct each false statement in the space below.

1. For best control of both the accelerator and brake pedals, rest the heel of your foot on the floor.   T   F

_____

2. To keep from rolling back after stopping on an uphill grade, use your right foot to press on the brake pedal while gently accelerating with your left foot.   T   F

_____

3. Threshold braking increases braking efficiency by locking the car's wheels in an emergency braking situation.   T   F

_____

4. The amount of braking pressure required to stop a vehicle depends in part upon the surface of the road.   T   F

_____

C. FIND OUT MORE. The chapter suggests purchasing a vehicle with antilock brakes. Call up a new vehicle dealer and ask if antilock brakes are an option with new vehicles; if so, how much do they cost?

_____

_____

_____

Speed Control

A. Complete the sentences below by filling in the blanks with the correct words.

1. The rate of acceleration is the _____ it takes to accelerate from one speed to another.

2. You check your speed by giving quick glances at the _____.

3. As _____ varies, there is a difference in the car's vibration and level of sound.

B. Complete the following statements by circling the correct words in the parentheses.

1. (Gradual/Sudden) acceleration is recommended in most cases.

2. As the speed of a vehicle increases, the rate of acceleration is (higher/lower).

3. You need (more/less) time to pass another vehicle when traveling at 50 mph than at 30 mph.

4. A heavy truck needs (more/less) time and distance to decelerate than cars do.

C. For each sentence below, circle T if the statement is true and F if it is false. Correct each false statement in the space below.

1. One of the factors that affects a car's acceleration rate is the road surface.   T   F

_____

2. Accelerating quickly saves fuel.   T   F

_____

3. For best control while accelerating, you should press gently on the accelerator with the heel of your foot.   T   F

_____

4. It is safe to look at the speedometer while driving as long as you do it by taking quick glances.   T   F

_____

D. FIND OUT MORE. The next time you are a passenger in a vehicle, try to judge the speed at which you are traveling. Write down your estimate on a piece of paper, and ask the driver to glance down at the speedometer and tell you the correct speed. Attempt this task at least five times. How often were you correct? Did you find that your estimates became more accurate with practice? Write your findings below.

_____

_____

STUDY GUIDE FOR CHAPTER 5   LESSON 3

Using a Manual Transmission

A. Correct each of the following statements. You do not have to repeat the sentence exactly.

1. When you make a downshift in an emergency, the first thing to do after you have pressed on the brake is to shift to Second gear.

_____

_____

2. The difference between driving an automatic vehicle and one with a manual transmission is that a manual shift requires the use of the clutch pedal to make the brakes work.

_____

_____

3. The friction point is the point at which the clutch and other parts of the engine separate.

_____

_____

4. You hold a manual transmission vehicle in place on a hill by pressing on the gas pedal slightly while keeping the clutch near the friction point.

_____

_____

5. The easiest way to get a feel for where the friction point is to practice using Fourth or Fifth gear.

_____

6. Glance at your feet from time to time as you are driving to be sure that they are on the correct pedals.

_____

_____

B. FIND OUT MORE. Ask at least ten people you know who drive whether they prefer an automatic or a manual transmission. What reasons do they give for their choices?

_____

_____

_____

_____

Steering a Vehicle

A. For each sentence below, circle T if the statement is true and F if it is false. Correct each false statement in the space below.

1. It often takes more time and energy to brake to avoid hitting an object than to steer away from it.   T   F

_____

2. At speeds over 25 or 30 mph, the only way to avoid a collision may be to step on the brakes.   T   F

_____

3. Keeping your vehicle moving on the path of travel you have chosen is called tracking.   T   F

_____

4. To track smoothly, you need to focus your attention directly in front of the vehicle you are driving.   T   F

_____

5. Steering through a turn requires more steering wheel movement than does lane positioning.   T   F

_____

6. In push-pull-feed steering, you have to cross your hands when turning the steering wheel.   T   F

_____

7. Backing while looking into the rearview mirror is not a good idea.   T   F

_____

8. When backing, the rear of your vehicle moves in the opposite direction to the steering wheel.   T   F

_____

B. FIND OUT MORE. Talk with somebody who drives frequently or with a professional driver such as a trucker, police officer, or bus driver. Ask the person what procedures she or he uses when backing up. What differences are there between the person's procedures and the one described in the chapter?

_____

_____

_____

CHAPTER 6 Basic Maneuvers

STUDY GUIDE FOR CHAPTER 6   LESSON 1

Moving into and out of Traffic

A. Read the following account of a collision. You are the investigating police officer. Make a sketch of the collision scene in the space below. Explain how the collision could have been avoided.

Vehicle A was parked alongside the right curb just behind vehicle B. The driver of vehicle A came out of the dry cleaner's and hung the dry-cleaned clothes over the left rear window. The driver entered vehicle A and checked for traffic in the rearview mirror. Seeing none, the driver began to move the vehicle away from the curb and into the traffic lane. Vehicle C, traveling in the same direction and coming from behind vehicle A, crashed into the driver's side of vehicle A. The impact pushed vehicle A into the left side of vehicle B.

_____

_____

_____

_____

B. FIND OUT MORE. Observe as a passenger in a car, bus, other vehicle, or even as a pedestrian, how people move from curb to curb. Keep notes on how the drivers that you observe manage visibility, time, and space. Can you draw any conclusions?

_____

_____

_____

_____

_____

_____

Right and Left Turns

A. Use a pencil or colored pencil to draw the path of each vehicle's intersection maneuver.

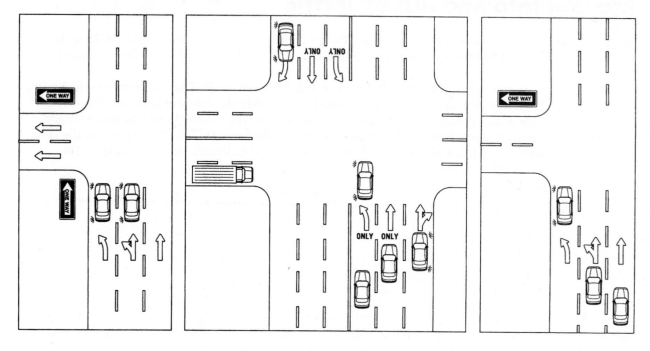

B. Complete the following sentences by filling in the correct word in the space below.

1. A driver turning left must _____ right-of-way to any cross traffic and to oncoming traffic.

2. When you are at an intersection and waiting to turn, your front wheels should be

_____.

3. You should signal your intentions to turn at least _____ feet in advance.

4. When turning left from a two-way street onto a two-way street, you should have a 9-second

gap in traffic to your right and a _____-second gap to your left.

5. When turning left from a two-way street, _____ your car near the center line.

C. FIND OUT MORE. Check out an intersection near where you live. What signs and markings give special information about turns, such as whether or not turns are allowed, or in which directions you can turn? Describe them below.

_____

_____

_____

STUDY GUIDE FOR CHAPTER 6   LESSON 3

Steering in Reverse and Making Turnabouts

A. For each sentence below, circle T if the statement is true and F if it is false. Correct each false statement in the space below.

1. The safest turnabout is the three-point turn.   T   F

_____

2. You should have at least 500 feet of visibility before you do a turnabout.   T   F

_____

3. A three-point turn should be made when the street is narrow and there are no driveways to turn into.   T   F

_____

4. A good location for three-point turn is on a curve.   T   F

_____

5. Driving around the block is often the easiest turnabout to make.   T   F

_____

6. U-turns may not be legal in all areas.   T   F

_____

7. You should not make a turnabout within 100 feet of an intersection.   T   F

_____

8. A two-point turnabout heading into a driveway on the right is considered dangerous.   T   F

_____

B. FIND OUT MORE. Are U-turns legal in your state? See if you can find the answer in your state driver's manual. See also if there are any restrictions on where you can and cannot make U-turns.

_____

_____

_____

_____

_____

_____

_____

Parking

A. For each sentence below, circle T if the statement is true and F if it is false. Correct each false statement in the space below.

1. Angled parking spaces are set at an angle of 30 to 90 degrees to the curb or line.   T   F

_____

2. When angle parking, stay at least 10 feet away from parked vehicles to give yourself room to maneuver.   T   F

_____

3. To parallel park, you need a space at least 10 feet longer than the length of your vehicle.   T   F

_____

4. It is a good idea not to park your vehicle next to a poorly parked vehicle.   T   F

_____

5. When parking downhill at a curb, park your vehicle with the wheels turned sharply to the left.   T   F

_____

6. When parking your vehicle downhill, leave it in Neutral if it has a manual transmission.   T   F

_____

7. When parking uphill next to a curb, park your vehicle with the wheels turned sharply to the left.   T   F

_____

8. If you are parking your vehicle uphill where there is no curb, your wheels should be turned sharply to the left.   T   F

_____

B. FIND OUT MORE. Find the following answers to parking questions in your state driver's manual.

1. Is it illegal to park at a bus stop? _____

2. Is it illegal to park in a loading zone? _____

3. How close to a fire hydrant can you park? _____

4. Can you park across someone else's driveway? _____

Safe Driving Procedures for Passing and Being Passed

A. For each sentence below, circle T if the statement is true and F if it is false. Correct each false statement in the space below.

1. You should not pass another vehicle in heavy fog.   T   F

   _____

2. You typically need to accelerate 25 miles per hour faster than the vehicle ahead of you if you are passing it on a two-lane highway.   T   F

   _____

3. You should exceed the speed limit only when passing a vehicle on a two-lane road.   T   F

   _____

4. If you are driving a vehicle at 50 mph, it will take you about 6 seconds to pass another vehicle that is going 40 mph.   T   F

   _____

5. You should signal your intent to return to the right lane when passing a vehicle after you see both headlights in your sideview mirror.   T   F

   _____

6. It is illegal to accelerate when you are being passed by another vehicle.   T   F

   _____

B. FIND OUT MORE. Pay careful attention to the route from your home to your school. Are there any no-passing zones on this route? What is the evidence that they are no-passing zones? Why do you think they are there?

Location	Evidence	Reason

CHAPTER 7 Searching and Giving Meaning

STUDY GUIDE FOR CHAPTER 7   LESSON 1

Sight

A. Match the following terms by placing the letter of the clue in the right column next to the item in the left column.

_____ **1.** visual acuity

_____ **2.** field of vision

_____ **3.** area of central vision

_____ **4.** peripheral vision

_____ **5.** depth perception

_____ **6.** distance judgment

a. gives three-dimensional perspective to objects

b. estimating distance between yourself and an object

c. ability to see clearly

d. what you see looking straight ahead and at an angle to the left and right

e. vision clearest in a narrow cone-shaped area directly in front of you

f. enables you to notice objects and movement to the side

B. For each sentence below, circle T if the statement is true and F if it is false. Correct each false statement in the space below.

1. About 90 percent of all decisions that you make while driving are based on information gathered with your eyes.   T   F

_____

2. A color-blind person cannot legally drive.   T   F

_____

3. When driving at night, you should increase your following distance to 1 second.   T   F

_____

4. You should switch on your high beams in city traffic.   T   F

_____

5. The light from an oncoming vehicle's headlights cause your eyes' pupils to become larger.   T   F

_____

C. FIND OUT MORE. Look in your state driver's manual. What visual acuity do you need to pass the vision test? What can be done to get your license if your visual acuity is low?

_____

_____

_____

Sound, Balance, and Touch

A. Match the Key Term on the left with its definition on the right.

_____ **1.** backward pitch

_____ **2.** forward pitch

_____ **3.** roll

_____ **4.** yaw

a. the spinning action resulting from the back tire sliding sideways toward the front tire

b. a transfer of weight to the rear of a vehicle; the result of rapid acceleration.

c. the feeling that occurs after a vehicle goes through a left-right combination turn on a corner.

d. a transfer of weight to the front of the vehicle; the result of rapid deceleration.

B. For each sentence below, circle T if the statement is true and F if it is false. Correct each false statement in the space below.

1. The sense of hearing is not crucial for driving successfully.   T   F

_____

2. Drivers with hearing loss can compensate by wearing hearing aids and relying more on their sense of vision.   T   F

_____

3. If you begin a turn by quickly and sharply turning the wheel, the vehicle will roll only a little and will remain stable throughout the turn.   T   F

_____

4. Sudden steering or braking maneuvers affect rear-vehicle balance and may result in the loss of tire traction.   T   F

_____

5. Out-of-balance tires cause increased wear on all steering and suspension components.   T   F

_____

C. FIND OUT MORE. The next time you are in a vehicle, take notes on the types and number of sounds you hear. How will paying attention to these sounds make you a better driver? What information do the sounds communicate?

_____

_____

_____

_____

Scanning, Searching, and Sensing

A. For each topic sentence below, give examples of how you would apply scanning, searching, and sensing. Imagine that you are actually driving. What will you be specifically looking for and doing?

Look ahead, not down.

_____

_____

Keep your eyes moving.

_____

_____

Get the big picture.

_____

_____

Make sure that others can see you.

_____

_____

Leave yourself a way out.

_____

_____

B. FIND OUT MORE. Interview someone you know who drives. Ask the person what information he or she collects about the road while driving in order to avoid collisions?

_____

_____

_____

_____

_____

_____

Giving Meaning

A. For each sentence below, circle T if the statement is true and F if it is false. Correct each false statement in the space below.

1. Giving meaning is a mental process that has to do with understanding what you perceive with your senses.   T   F

_____

2. Giving meaning requires your full, undivided attention while driving.   T   F

_____

3. Traffic situations are always predictable.   T   F

_____

4. Driving in familiar areas requires the same amount of attention as driving in less familiar areas.   T   F

_____

5. Commentary driving involves "saying" aloud what you sense in real-world traffic situations.   T   F

_____

B. List the five factors that affect your ability to give meaning to a driving scene.

1. _____

2. _____

3. _____

4. _____

5. _____

C. FIND OUT MORE. Imagine that you are driving on a crowded road and are about to make a left turn at a busy intersection. Develop a plan for giving meaning to events that might occur at the intersection (consider, for example, the possibility of pedestrians crossing the street against the light.) Include in your plan how to look, where to look, and what to look for.

_____

_____

_____

_____

CHAPTER 8 Options and Responses

STUDY GUIDE FOR CHAPTER 8   LESSON 1

Options and Choice

A. Match the Key Term on the left with its definition on the right.

_____ **1.** option   **a.** events that you expect might happen.

_____ **2.** comparison   **b.** a potential choice based on a driver's knowledge, experiences, and skills.

_____ **3.** assumption

_____ **4.** choice   **c.** the examination of similarities and dissimilarities to determine options.

     d. the selection of two or more possible options.

B. For each traffic situation below, list your options as a driver. Which option do you think is the best for each situation?

You are traveling at 45 mph, and the vehicle in front of you begins to slow down.

_____

_____

A vehicle is coming up quickly behind you and moves into one of your blind spots.

_____

_____

You are approaching an intersection, and the traffic signal is beginning to change from green to yellow.

_____

_____

C. FIND OUT MORE. Based on your experiences as a passenger in a motor vehicle, list the assumptions you make about right-of-way rules at a 4-way stop.

_____

_____

_____

Responses to Manage Space and Time

A. For each sentence below, circle T if the statement is true and F if it is false. Correct each false statement in the space below.

1. A driver must be aware of how much time and space it takes for a vehicle to react to a driving event.   T   F

_____

2. Human-perception time refers to the total time needed for a human being to determine his or her options in a driving situation and to choose one.   T   F

_____

3. As a driver, you can safely manage space and time by maintaining a constant speed regardless of traffic or road conditions.   T   F

_____

4. Driving with your low beams on during the daylight hours makes your vehicle visible about 220 feet sooner than when you drive without them.   T   F

_____

5. Road grime can reduce headlight illumination up to 50 percent.   T   F

_____

6. You should identify objects that could increase the level of risk 12 to 15 seconds ahead of you.   T   F

_____

7. If you double your speed, your stopping distance will double.   T   F

_____

B. FIND OUT MORE. Interview at least two people who you know are drivers. Ask them to recount a driving situation in which they managed time and space by either steering or accelerating. Do you think each driver made the correct choice? Why?

_____

_____

_____

_____

_____

_____

Managing Visibility

A. Match the Key Term on the left with its definition on the right.

_____ **1.** visual lead

_____ **2.** visual control zone

_____ **3.** response zone

_____ **4.** following interval

_____ **5.** potential immediate crash zone

a. the area directly in front and to the rear of your vehicle that will likely cause you to crash when a potential hazard becomes a real hazard.

b. the zone where you begin to respond to what you perceive.

c. the zone where you identify objects/conditions that may require a response or continuous attention.

d. the distance you can see ahead of your vehicle.

e. the safe amount of time you should allow when following another vehicle or when being followed.

B. For each sentence below, circle T if the statement is true and F if it is false. Correct each false statement in the space below.

1. Maintaining adequate space around your vehicle is the best way to avoid collisions.   T   F

_____

2. To maintain an adequate visual lead margin, scan and search 50 to 60 seconds ahead of your vehicle.   T   F

_____

3. The visual control zone begins 5 to 10 seconds ahead of your vehicle.   T   F

_____

4. In the response zone, you take actions that will control or reduce perceived risks.   T   F

_____

5. The potential immediate crash zone is about 6 to 8 seconds ahead of your vehicle.   T   F

_____

6. To reduce the possibility of a collision, you should always be able to stop within the distance that you can see ahead of your vehicle.   T   F

_____

C. FIND OUT MORE. During the next week, observe other people's driving while you are riding in the school bus or in another vehicle. Are people keeping safe following intervals?

_____

_____

_____

Margins of Safety

A. For each sentence below, circle T if the statement is true and F if it is false. Correct each false statement in the space below.

1. Keeping a margin of safety allows you the space, time, and visibility for safe movements at any time.   T   F

_____

2. The margin of safety is a fixed distance of 10 to 15 seconds ahead of your vehicle.   T   F

_____

3. You increase risk by allowing space between your vehicle and another.   T   F

_____

4. You should keep a minimum of 3 seconds of following distance, and 4 to 5 seconds at speeds of 40 mph or more.   T   F

_____

5. Always try to have at least one car width of space to one side of your car.   T   F

_____

B. List five circumstances in which you should increase the margin of safety around your vehicle.

_____

_____

_____

_____

_____

C. FIND OUT MORE. Using three separate driving situations, record your observations on the ways other drivers handle margins of safety when changing lanes. Where were you? What time of the day was it? Could a collision have occurred because of what you saw?

_____

_____

_____

_____

_____

_____

CHAPTER 9 Environments and Traffic Settings

STUDY GUIDE FOR CHAPTER 9   LESSON 1

Residential Streets

A. Complete the following statements by circling the correct words in parentheses.

1. Residential streets are found in (downtown urban areas/neighborhoods).

2. Driving at (faster/slower) speeds is essential on residential streets.

3. (Always/Sometimes) yield to pedestrians at intersections, whether or not crosswalks are painted on the street.

4. When driving on residential streets, slow down (more than usual/less than usual) if your visibility is poor.

5. Unless otherwise posted, the legal speed limit on residential streets is usually (25 mph/35 mph).

6. Children are the (secondary/primary) pedestrians on residential streets.

7. (Always use/Avoid using) residential streets as shortcuts.

8. Most collisions occur (close to/far from) home.

9. If you are on the side of a residential street with parked cars, you (are/are not) required to pull in behind those cars and wait for oncoming traffic to pass.

B. FIND OUT MORE. Observe a residential street for one hour, and keep a log of potential hazards that you notice (e.g., children playing in the street or a vehicle backing out of a driveway). If you were driving at the time, what actions would you take to reduce the risk of potential hazards?

_____

_____

_____

_____

_____

_____

_____

_____

_____

Urban and Suburban Streets

A. What are the guidelines for managing visibility, time, and space in urban and suburban driving? Write at least three guidelines in each category.

Visibility

_____

_____

Time

_____

_____

_____

Space

_____

_____

_____

B. What special factors affect urban and suburban driving?

_____

_____

_____

C. FIND OUT MORE. The chapter lists some clues that indicate when the behavior of other drivers could be a potential problem or danger to you. What are they? Why would the actions listed be a hazard? During the next week, see how many of these clues you can spot. Report your findings below.

_____

_____

_____

_____

_____

_____

_____

STUDY GUIDE FOR CHAPTER 9   LESSON 3

Multiple-Lane Expressways

A. Finish each sentence below. Give as complete information as you can.

1. A limited-access, or controlled-access, highway allows vehicles to enter or to exit _____

_____

2. An expressway is a divided highway with limited access that has more than one lane _____

_____

3. A turnpike is a road or highway that requires drivers to _____

_____

4. A beltway is a highway that goes around _____

_____

5. A parkway is a wide, landscaped highway that may be limited _____

_____

6. A deceleration lane allows vehicles _____

_____

7. An acceleration lane lets vehicles _____

_____

8. An interchange is a place where vehicles can _____

_____

B. FIND OUT MORE. Go to the library and look at a road atlas. Where are the limited-access roads in your state? Where do any interstate highways enter the state, and what routes do they take? How can you tell whether a road is a toll road by looking at the atlas?

_____

_____

_____

_____

_____

_____

STUDY GUIDE FOR CHAPTER 9   LESSON 4

Rural Roads

A. In the following sentences, two word choices are given. Circle the correct one.

1. Traffic is generally (heavier/lighter) on country roads.

2. Country roads generally have (higher/lower) speed limits than city roads.

3. Country roads have (more/fewer) traffic lights then city streets.

4. The greater risk of colliding with another vehicle is in the (country/city).

5. There is a greater risk of your car colliding with a fixed object in the (country/city).

6. If you are coming close to a rider on horseback, you (should/should not) use your horn to warn the rider.

B. For each sentence below, circle T if the statement is true and F if it is false. Correct each false statement in the space below.

1. Trees and shrubs growing near the roadway can limit visibility.   T   F

_____

2. All country roads have shoulders.   T   F

_____

3. In the country, you should not drive with your headlights on during the day.   T   F

_____

4. When approaching an animal near the road, you should drive slowly.   T   F

_____

5. Never pass on an uphill grade when you don't have a clear path ahead.   T   F

_____

C. FIND OUT MORE. Call your local law enforcement agency, your state patrol, or a local insurance agent. Ask them what they think the major differences are between city and country driving. Ask them where they think fatal collisions are more likely to occur, and why. Report your findings below.

_____

_____

_____

_____

_____

CHAPTER 10 Intersections

STUDY GUIDE FOR CHAPTER 10   LESSON 1

Basic Intersections

A. For each sentence below, circle T if the statement is true and F if it is false. Correct each false statement in the space below.

1. Places where one road meets or crosses another are called intersections.   T   F

_____

2. Intersections are usually controlled by traffic lights.   T   F

_____

3. When approaching an intersection with a 4-way stop, assume that all drivers will obey the right-of-way rules.   T   F

_____

4. Before entering an intersection, scan and search all four corners to make sure nothing will block your route.   T   F

_____

5. If you are approaching an intersection and the light begins to change from yellow to red, speed up to make it across the intersection.   T   F

_____

6. A T-intersection is created when one road ends and forms a "T" with a crossroad.   T   F

_____

7. At a T-intersection, you must yield to all traffic on the cross street.   T   F

_____

B. FIND OUT MORE. From the sidewalk, observe a four-way intersection in your neighborhood. Note the width of the cross street, and practice the counting method for determining when it is safe to enter and to cross the intersection. How often and in what situations would you need more than an 8-second gap to cross safely? Note your findings below.

_____

_____

_____

_____

Railroad Crossings

A. For each sentence below, circle T if the statement is true and F if it is false. Correct each false statement in the space below.

1. When you come to any railroad crossing, you should always slow down.   T   F

_____

2. You should stop no closer than 5 feet from a railroad crossing.   T   F

_____

3. If the lights at a railroad crossing are flashing, you can cross the tracks only if you do not see a train and after looking carefully.   T   F

_____

4. A railroad crossing with no lights flashing does not necessarily mean that it is safe to cross without looking first.   T   F

_____

5. You should stop on railroad tracks only if the vehicle ahead of you has stopped.   T   F

_____

6. As soon as a train has passed, you should look and listen to see if there is another train before moving.   T   F

_____

7. If your car has stalled on the tracks of a railroad crossing and you see a train coming, leave your vehicle at once and move away from the tracks.   T   F

_____

8. Never assume that a track is clear or that you can beat a train.   T   F

_____

B. FIND OUT MORE. Choose a nearby railroad crossing and describe it in as much detail as you can. Are the warning signs leading up to it adequate and visible? How far ahead of the crossing are the signs? Does the crossing have a gate and warning lights? Overall, in your opinion, is it a safe crossing?

_____

_____

_____

_____

STUDY GUIDE FOR CHAPTER 10   LESSON 3

Roundabouts

A. Complete the sentences below by filling in the blanks with the correct words.

1. When approaching a roundabout, _____ as you approach the traffic circle.

2. If other vehicles are in the roundabout, _____ to traffic until you can enter.

3. Before entering a roundabout, scan for pedestrians and _____.

4. Go in the _____ of traffic once you're in a roundabout.

5. Traffic movement in a roundabout is always _____.

6. Unless otherwise posted, the speed in a roundabout is generally _____ or less.

7. Two-lane roundabouts allow for a _____ volume of traffic than do single-lane roundabouts.

8. _____ turns are completed by traveling around the center of the island.

9. Roundabouts move traffic through intersections at a _____ and

_____ pace.

10. All vehicles in a roundabout are required to yield to _____ in a crosswalk.

11. Vehicles in the circulating lane have the _____.

B. FIND OUT MORE. Use the Internet to research the history of roundabouts in the United States. Are roundabouts used to control traffic at intersections in your state? What benefits have the use of roundabouts brought to traffic control in your state? Have there been any disadvantages. Report your findings below.

_____

_____

_____

_____

_____

_____

_____

Complex Intersections

A. For each sentence below, circle T if the statement is true and F if it is false. Correct each false statement in the space below.

1. A complex intersection is one where two major roadways cross paths.   T   F

_____

2. A complex intersection can contain five to six lanes, multiple turning lanes, and turn-arrow signals.   T   F

_____

3. Very few collisions take place in complex intersections.   T   F

_____

4. Side-impact collisions occur when a vehicle is hit by another vehicle from the side.   T   F

_____

5. The majority of side-impact collisions occur at intersections.   T   F

_____

6. Fewer than half of rear-end crashes take place at or near intersections.   T   F

_____

B. What electronic signals and body gestures can you use to communicate with pedestrians and other drivers at complex intersections?

_____

_____

_____

_____

C. FIND OUT MORE. Research the collision statistics at complex intersections for your state. Report your findings below.

_____

_____

_____

STUDY GUIDE FOR CHAPTER 10   LESSON 5

Interchanges

A. Match the term on the left with its definition on the right.

_____ **1.** interchange

_____ **2.** through lanes

_____ **3.** speed-change lanes

_____ **4.** ramps

a. a place where one major freeway crosses another road

b. allow a vehicle to reduce speed to exit a freeway or to increase speed to merge into moving traffic

c. move vehicles from one road to another

d. designed for drivers staying on the same turnpike or interstate highway, these lanes continue straight through an interchange

B. In the space below, sketch an example of a cloverleaf, diamond, and trumpet interchange. List the main characteristics of each underneath your sketches.

Diamond	Cloverleaf	Trumpet

C. FIND OUT MORE. The next time you go on a trip in a motor vehicle, take note of the different types of interchanges on the freeway. Which type was most common? How were traffic patterns affected by each interchange?

_____

_____

_____

_____

CHAPTER 11   Sharing the Roadway with Others

STUDY GUIDE FOR CHAPTER 11   LESSON 1

Driving with Pedestrians and Animals

A. Drivers must be on the lookout for pedestrians who do not know or who ignore the rules of the road. Label each pedestrian error listed below with the letter in the picture that illustrates it.

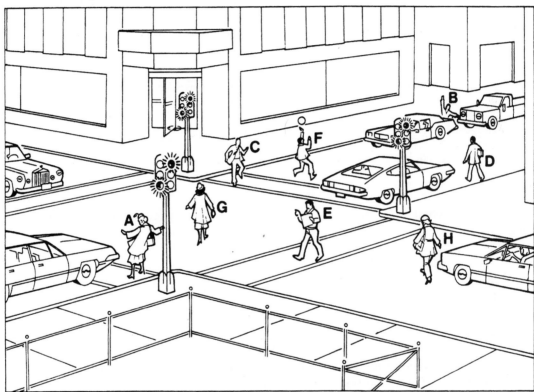

_____	**1.** Playing in the street		_____	**5.** Ignoring traffic
_____	**2.** Taking a shortcut from sidewalk to corner		_____	**6.** Walking in traffic when intoxicated
_____	**3.** Crossing between intersections		_____	**7.** Walking diagonally across an intersection
_____	**4.** Stepping out from between parked vehicles		_____	**8.** Crossing against a signal

B. FIND OUT MORE. Ask ten people who drive often what they do when they see an animal in the road. What action do they take to avoid hitting it? Sometimes colliding with an animal when driving is unavoidable. If any of the people you talk to have had this experience, ask them what happened and what they did.

_____

_____

_____

Driving with Bicycles and Motorcycles

A. For each sentence below, circle T if the statement is true and F if it is false. Correct each false statement in the space below.

1. On the roadway, motorcycles are less visible than cars.   T   F

_____

2. When driving behind a cyclist, reduce your following distance.   T   F

_____

3. The risk of a serious or fatal injury to a driver of a motorcycle involved in a collision is low.   T   F

_____

4. Since a motorcycle is smaller than a car, it is safe to pass one in a tight space.   T   F

_____

5. Two-wheeled vehicles are most difficult to spot when they approach from behind on a highway.   T   F

_____

6. Motorcyclists have the same rights and responsibilities on public roadways as automobile drivers.   T   F

_____

B. FIND OUT MORE. Look through local newspapers for a week, collecting as many articles as possible about bicycle and motorcycle collisions. What were the causes? Was weather a factor? What were the results?

_____

_____

_____

_____

_____

_____

_____

_____

STUDY GUIDE FOR CHAPTER 11   LESSON 3

Driving with Light Trucks and Small Vehicles

A. For each sentence below, circle T if the statement is true and F if it is false. Correct each false statement in the space below.

   1. Drivers of pickups, sport utility vehicles, or vans can see farther ahead than drivers of cars.   T   F

_____

   2. Vehicles driving behind a pickup, sport utility vehicle, or van will have no trouble seeing ahead. T   F

_____

   3. Driving a light truck can make you more tired than driving a car.   T   F

_____

   4. Higher headlights on a sport utility vehicle can cause more glare.   T   F

_____

   5. The center of gravity is lower on light trucks.   T   F

_____

   6. Light trucks tend to be easier to drive in heavy winds because they are bigger than cars.   T   F

_____

   7. When driving a small, low-powered vehicle, you should allow extra space and time to pass another vehicle.   T   F

_____

   8. If you see an emergency vehicle with its lights flashing, you should pull to the left and let it pass.   T   F

_____

B. FIND OUT MORE. In some states, you must stop for an ice cream truck that has lights flashing. Look at your state driver's manual, or any other resource that you can find, and see what the law says about this.

_____

_____

_____

_____

Driving with Large Vehicles

A. For each sentence below, circle T if the statement is true and F if it is false. Correct each false statement in the space below.

1. Trucks on the road today can be up to 60 feet long.   T   F

_____

2. Truck drivers have excellent visibility ahead.   T   F

_____

3. A truck tends to lose speed when going downhill.   T   F

_____

4. You should decrease your following distance when driving behind a truck.   T   F

_____

5. You should pass a truck on the right side of the roadway.   T   F

_____

6. You should use the 2-second rule when following a bus.   T   F

_____

7. You can manage the added risk of driving with larger vehicles by increasing your following distance to give you more time to maneuver and stop.   T   F

_____

B. FIND OUT MORE. Look at your state driver's manual. What does it say about tractor-trailers? Do people need a special license to drive a tractor-trailer? Are there any speed limits that are different for tractor-trailers? What other regulations about tractor-trailers does your driver's manual discuss?

_____

_____

_____

_____

_____

_____

_____

CHAPTER 12 | Vehicle Movement

Using Appropriate Speed

A. Imagine that you are driving and would like to change lanes. To determine if you are driving at an appropriate speed to make the maneuver, ask yourself the following questions. After each question, write an explanation of why it is an important consideration.

1. What is the path of travel like in the lane you are in? _____

_____

2. What is the path of travel like in the lane you want to enter? _____

_____

3. Are other vehicles signaling to move into the lane you want to enter? _____

_____

4. What is happening in the lanes behind you? _____

_____

5. How fast are you going? Can you change lanes without exceeding the speed limit? _____

_____

6. Do you have room to make the move safely? _____

_____

7. How much of a gap is there between vehicles in the lane you are moving into? _____

_____

_____

B. FIND OUT MORE. Using three separate situations, record your observations on the ways other drivers handle determining appropriate speed when changing lanes. Where were you? What time of day was it? Could a collision have occurred because of what you saw?

_____

_____

_____

_____

STUDY GUIDE FOR CHAPTER 12   LESSON 2

Total Stopping Distance

A. For each sentence below, circle T if the statement is true and F if it is false. Correct each false statement in the space below.

1. The amount of distance you need to stop the car increases with speed.   T   F

_____

2. If you double your speed, you will need four times the distance to stop.   T   F

_____

3. Vehicle-braking distance is the distance your vehicle travels after you see a problem and before you apply the brakes.   T   F

_____

4. Total stopping distance is the distance it takes from the moment you see a problem until your vehicle is stopped.   T   F

_____

5. A 3,000-pound vehicle traveling at 60 mph will require about 300 to 500 feet to stop.
T   F

_____

6. If a vehicle is tailgating you or a large vehicle is behind you, identify a path for evasive steering.   T   F

_____

7. The condition of the road surface affects total stopping distance.   T   F

_____

B. FIND OUT MORE. During the next week, observe other people's driving while you are riding in the school bus or another vehicle. Are drivers keeping enough space between their vehicles to allow for the total stopping distance?

_____

_____

_____

_____

_____

Natural Laws and the Movement of Your Vehicle

A. Match the following terms by placing the letter of the definition or a description of what the item does to the left of the item.

_____ **1.** inertia

_____ **2.** friction

_____ **3.** traction

_____ **4.** momentum

_____ **5.** kinetic energy

_____ **6.** center of gravity

a. friction between your tires and the road

b. energy of motion

c. causes objects to continue moving in a straight line

d. the point about which weight is evenly distributed

e. force between two surfaces that resists the movement of one surface across the other

f. the product of weight and speed

B. Complete the following sentences by writing in the natural law each sentence is describing.

1. When you brake quickly and your books and packages on the backseat fall onto the floor, the

force at work is _____.

2. The force that makes your tires "stick" to the surface of the road is called _____.

3. Two vehicles going at the same speed hit the same brick wall, but the one that weighs more

sustains much more damage. This is an example of _____.

4. The faster a vehicle moves, the more _____ energy it has.

5. The force that slows your vehicle going uphill is called _____.

C. FIND OUT MORE. What is kinetic energy? Look in your library and find out more about what the effects of kinetic energy are. Summarize your findings below.

_____

_____

_____

_____

_____

_____

_____

Natural Laws and Steering and Braking

A. For each sentence below, circle T if the statement is true and F if it is false. Correct each false statement in the space below.

1. Perception distance, reaction distance, and braking distance make up total stopping distance.   T   F

_____

2. Braking is a result of friction between the brake linings and your foot.   T   F

_____

3. Braking distance is greater on a smooth road.   T   F

_____

4. Your braking distance decreases if you are going downhill.   T   F

_____

5. Your ability to steer a vehicle depends partly upon the condition of the vehicle's suspension.   T   F

_____

6. Directional control is a vehicle's ability to hold a straight line.   T   F

_____

7. A banked road is higher on the inside of curves than on the outside.   T   F

_____

8. A crowned road is higher in the center of the road than on the edges.   T   F

_____

B. FIND OUT MORE. Go to the library. Look up centrifugal force and centripetal force. What are they, and what are the differences between them?

_____

_____

_____

_____

_____

_____

_____

CHAPTER 13   Light and Weather Conditions

STUDY GUIDE FOR CHAPTER 13   LESSON 1

Driving Safely in Low Light and at Night

A. For each sentence below, circle T if the statement is true and F if it is false. Correct each false statement in the space below.

1. As visibility decreases, your risk of being in an accident decreases.   T   F

_____

2. Headlights from an oncoming vehicle can have a blinding effect.   T   F

_____

3. When driving during dusk and dawn hours, you should use your parking lights.   T   F

_____

4. At night, you should decrease the distance between your vehicle and the vehicle ahead.   T   F

_____

5. You can use your high beams on dark roads when there are no other vehicles around.   T   F

_____

6. When an oncoming vehicle's headlights are bright, you should look directly at the headlights.   T   F

_____

7. At night, you should not overdrive your headlights.   T   F

_____

8. At dusk, you should keep your low-beam headlights on.   T   F

_____

9. Overdriving your headlights means driving at a speed that will not allow you to stop within their range.   T   F

_____

10. At night, you should get into the habit of looking for objects beyond your headlight beams.   T   F

_____

B. FIND OUT MORE. Keep a record of all traffic collisions reported in your local newspaper for one week. What percentage of the collisions happened between the hours of 9 p.m. and 6 a.m.?

_____

_____

STUDY GUIDE FOR CHAPTER 13   LESSON 2

Visibility, Bright Light, and Glare

A. For each sentence below, circle T if the statement is true and F if it is false. Correct each false statement in the space below.

1. The sun's glare is most dangerous to drivers at noon.   T   F

_____

2. A badly scratched windshield should be replaced.   T   F

_____

3. Sunglasses are not effective against the glare of late afternoon sun.   T   F

_____

4. During periods of extreme glare, you should decrease your following distance.   T   F

_____

5. Driving with your low-beam headlights on does not help when the glare is strong.   T   F

_____

B. What advance preparation can you make before driving when you know that you may be driving in glaring sun?

_____

_____

_____

_____

C. FIND OUT MORE. Call a local optometrist's office, the optical department of a local store, or a vision clinic, and ask what are some of the best kinds of sunglasses made to combat the effects of the sun's glare. Ask how much they cost. Report your findings below.

_____

_____

_____

_____

_____

_____

STUDY GUIDE FOR CHAPTER 13   LESSON 3

Minimizing Risk in Rain and Snow

A. For each sentence below, circle T if the statement is true and F if it is false. Correct each false statement in the space below.

1. When driving in snow, you should follow the tire tracks of the vehicle ahead of you because the tracks are drier and give better traction.   T   F

_____

2. Driving with snow tires increases fuel economy.   T   F

_____

3. To prevent skids, you should change speeds as rapidly as possible.   T   F

_____

4. Roads are not very slick during the first 15 minutes of a rainfall.   T   F

_____

5. Hydroplaning happens when your vehicle rides on a thin film of water.   T   F

_____

B. If your vehicle became stuck in the snow, what would you do to set it free?

_____

_____

_____

_____

C. FIND OUT MORE. Most states that allow the use of studded snow tires have restrictions on when they can be used. What does your state's driver's manual say about this?

_____

_____

_____

_____

_____

_____

_____

STUDY GUIDE FOR CHAPTER 13   LESSON 4

Other Hazardous Weather Conditions

A. What precautions should you take when driving in fog? What should you do when fog becomes very dense?

_____

_____

_____

_____

_____

_____

B. What are the dangers of driving in high wind? What can you do to drive more safely in very windy situations?

_____

_____

_____

_____

_____

_____

C. FIND OUT MORE. The chapter says that in fog, your vehicle can collect moisture on the inside as well as on the outside of its windows. What can you do to prevent this? Visit or call a local auto parts store and ask if there are any products on the market that reduce moisture on the inside of your vehicle's windows.

_____

_____

_____

_____

_____

_____

CHAPTER 14 Environmental Challenges

STUDY GUIDE FOR CHAPTER 14   LESSON 1

Hill and Mountain Driving

A. Complete the sentences below by filling in the blanks with the correct words.

1. When you drive downhill, _____ makes you go faster.

2. If you are behind a truck when going downhill, _____ your following distance.

3. When going from a flat highway to driving uphill, your vehicle needs _____ power to maintain the same speed.

4. Going up a hill in a vehicle equipped with a manual transmission means that you have to

   _____ to gain power.

5. As you drive downhill in a vehicle equipped with manual transmission, you may want to

   _____ to help your vehicle slow down.

6. In high altitudes, there is _____ oxygen in the air.

7. In high altitudes, a vehicle's engine may stall because at that altitude, gas can

   _____.

B. For driving on mountain roads, what are the differences between automatic and manual transmissions? What are some special problems that mountains present because of their high altitudes?

   _____

   _____

   _____

   _____

   _____

C. FIND OUT MORE. Go to the library and look at a topographical road map of your state. Where are the roads in your state with the highest elevations? If your state has no roads at higher elevations, look at another state.

   _____

   _____

   _____

Skids

A. Complete the following sentences.

1. A _____ skid occurs when a tire suddenly loses pressure.

2. A _____ skid occurs when you apply the brakes so hard that one or more wheels lock.

3. When driving on slick roads, you should make _____ and smooth changes in your speed.

4. When _____ is reduced, your tires lose their grip on the road's surface.

5. The kind of skid in which you lose steering control while making a turn is called a

   _____ skid.

6. A _____ skid occurs when you press on the accelerator suddenly, too hard.

B. What is the correct and safe way to steer out of a skid?

_____

_____

_____

_____

C. FIND OUT MORE. Talk with someone whose job involves a lot of driving. Ask this person to describe what happens when a driver brakes in a skid. Diagram what happens in the space below.

_____

_____

_____

_____

_____

_____

_____

STUDY GUIDE FOR CHAPTER 14   LESSON 3

Avoiding or Minimizing Crash Damage

A. For each pair of vehicles, put an X next to the one that would experience the greater force of impact in a collision.

_____ **1.** Vehicle A is moving at 35 mph.

_____ Vehicle B is moving at 45 mph.

_____ **2.** Truck X hits a tree.

_____ Truck Y hits a wooden fence.

_____ **3.** Vehicle Y is carrying five passengers.

_____ Vehicle C is carrying only the driver.

_____ **4.** Motorcycle A runs into a haystack.

_____ Motorcycle B runs into a concrete divider.

B. With a ruler, measure the tread depth of some tires in your neighborhood or at school. Make sure that you have the permission of the owners to do this. What percentage of cars had all four tires with a tread depth of at least 1/16 inch? How many cars had tread depths of between 1/16 and 1/8 inch?

_____

_____

_____

_____

C. FIND OUT MORE. The chapter briefly discusses what an antilock brake system (ABS) is. Use any resource that you can find, such as a mechanic, literature from the library, or an advertisement. Find out as much as you can about an antilock brake system. How does it work? How much extra does it cost? Would you want one in your vehicle?

_____

_____

_____

_____

_____

_____

Challenging Environmental Factors

A. For each sentence below, circle T if the statement is true and F if it is false. If the statement is false, correct it in the space below.

1. Decreased visibility makes it easier to judge distances.   T   F

_____

2. Bad weather can reduce the ability of your tires to grip the road.   T   F

_____

3. When driving on snow or ice, it is essential to change direction quickly to minimize the risk of skidding.   T   F

_____

4. Roads are the slickest in the early part of a rainstorm because the moisture mixes with dirt and oil on the road.   T   F

_____

5. The main thing you can do to prevent hydroplaning is to drive slowly.   T   F

_____

6. Using your high-beam headlights is essential in fog.   T   F

_____

7. A strong gust of wind can push a vehicle out of its lane.   T   F

_____

8. When approaching a large vehicle on a slushy roadway, turn on your windshield wipers as you meet.   T   F

_____

9. Traction is the single most important factor in maintaining vehicle control.   T   F

_____

B. FIND OUT MORE. Research collision statistics for your state. How many collisions occurred in your state last year because of hydroplaning? What actions can you take to minimize the chance that hydroplaning will happen to you.

_____

_____

_____

CHAPTER 15 Vehicular Emergencies

STUDY GUIDE FOR CHAPTER 15   LESSON 1

Engine, Brake, and Steering Failures

A. The three procedures listed below are possible ways of slowing your car in case of total brake failure. Match each procedure with its result.

_____ **1.** Shift to a lower gear.

_____ **2.** Pump the brake pedal rapidly.

_____ **3.** Use the parking brake, keeping your hand on the release button or handle.

    a. slows the rear wheels

    b. slows the engine and forward movement of the vehicle

    c. may build up pressure in the brake-fluid lines

B. Suppose you have tried the above methods without success. Study the picture. Explain what you might do to stop yourself at each numbered spot if you were driving vehicle X and your brakes were not working. Then add one more emergency measure you might try.

1. _____

2. _____

3. _____

4. _____

5. Another measure to try when the brakes fail is:

_____

_____

_____

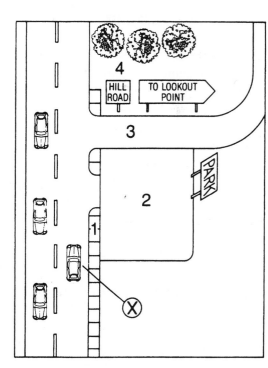

C. FIND OUT MORE. The chapter lists several emergency items to keep in the trunk of your vehicle. Ask someone you know who drives what her or his family keep in their vehicle for emergencies. How is this person's answer different from what the chapter lists?

_____

_____

_____

STUDY GUIDE FOR CHAPTER 15   LESSON 2

Tire Failure and Other Serious Problems

A. The following steps outline what you should do if a tire loses pressure, but they are in the wrong order. In the space next to each step, write a number to show where in the order it should appear.

_____ **a.** Check the traffic around you. When you find a gap, signal and steer off the roadway as far as you can.

_____ **b.** Get out of the vehicle, and have any passengers get out also.

_____ **c.** Keep a firm grip on the steering wheel with both hands.

_____ **d.** Shift into Park (or Reverse in a manual-shift vehicle), and put on your emergency flashers.

_____ **e.** Release the accelerator slowly. Don't brake.

B. For each sentence below, circle T if the statement is true and F if it is false. Correct each false statement in the space below.

1. Between 300 and 400 people are killed yearly while changing tires, when the vehicle falls off the jack or they are hit by other vehicles.   T   F

_____

2. An engine fire cannot be put out with water.   T   F

_____

3. Jump-starting a battery whose fluid is frozen can cause the battery to explode.   T   F

_____

4. Check the brake-fluid level once a month if you drive 10,000 miles or more a year.   T   F

_____

C. FIND OUT MORE. Tires are rated by their safety features to help you make good purchasing decisions. Go to a library and look up articles in Consumer Reports, or call a local tire store; find out what features tires are rated on, what the possible "grades" are, and what a good rating is. Summarize your findings below.

_____

_____

_____

_____

_____

_____

STUDY GUIDE FOR CHAPTER 15   LESSON 3

Waiting for Help and Protecting the Scene

A. Read the following paragraph that describes a situation in which a vehicle you are driving breaks down. In the space below the paragraph, write down what was done correctly under the "Right" heading and what was not correctly done, under "Wrong."

You are driving down the interstate highway when you notice your vehicle's temperature gauge beginning to climb. You decide to wait to see if it gets any worse. Finally, the temperature gets very high and you decide to pull over. You are now driving in a road construction area where there is very little shoulder available. You get out of your vehicle, tie a scarf on the right-hand side door handle, and open the vehicle's trunk. You then turn on the vehicle's emergency flashers, and since it is very cold outside, you get back into the vehicle and wait for help. You are careful to close the window all the way, since your heater is keeping you warm and you do not want to waste the heat. Soon someone sees you and pulls over. The person comes over to your vehicle, and you get out.

RIGHT	WRONG

B. FIND OUT MORE. Call a local emergency road service. Ask them about the costs associated with road service.

1. Do they bill insurance companies? _____

2. How much do they charge to fix a flat tire? _____

3. How much do they charge to help someone who runs out of gas? _____

4. How much is the towing charge per mile? _____

5. How much is the basic charge just to come to help somebody? _____

STUDY GUIDE FOR CHAPTER 15   LESSON 4

If You Are Involved in a Collision

A. You are driving at 55 mph in the right-hand lane of the freeway. Traffic ahead of you slows down to a near stop; since you see some highway construction warning signs, you figure that this is the reason for the slowdown. The vehicle directly behind you does not notice you slowing down and hits you from behind. You, in turn, hit the vehicle ahead of you. You are feeling fine, but your passenger says that her neck and back are hurting from the collision. The driver of the vehicle that hit you comes to your vehicle and acts very mad at you, saying that the accident was your fault because your brake lights were not working. What actions will you take at the accident scene, and in what order? What will you say to the driver of the vehicle that hit you?

_____

_____

_____

_____

_____

B. For each sentence below, circle T if the statement is true and F if it is false. Correct each false statement in the space below.

1. When a driver is involved in a collision, the driver should never move the vehicle until the police arrive.   T   F

_____

2. After a collision, reflective triangles should be set up no more than 50 feet in front of and behind a vehicle.   T   F

_____

3. If you are involved in a collision that results in serious injury or death, you must not leave the accident scene until the police allow you to go.   T   F

_____

4. People involved in a collision should be moved immediately out of their vehicles to a safe spot on the side of the road.   T   F

_____

C. FIND OUT MORE. Look at your state driver's manual. Under what conditions must you file an accident report?

_____

_____

_____

CHAPTER 16 Physical Readiness

STUDY GUIDE FOR CHAPTER 16   LESSON 1

Fatigue and Driving

A. For each sentence below, circle T if the statement is true and F if it is false. If the statement is false, correct it in the space below.

1. "Down time," or the time when people are less alert than usual, occurs for most people between the hours of 1 p.m. and 5 p.m.   T   F

_____

2. The best way to fight fatigue is to stop what you are doing and get some coffee.   T   F

_____

3. Having a steady flow of fresh air in your vehicle can help you fight fatigue.   T   F

_____

4. If you have to pull off the road at night, your windows should be lowered at least halfway to avoid carbon monoxide poisoning.   T   F

_____

5. A good plan to keep yourself alert while driving is to take 15-minute breaks every 2 hours.   T   F

_____

6. It is safe to drive for up to 15 hours a day.   T   F

_____

B. Fatigue is a major cause of accidents on the highways. Write in the spaces below what your personal plan will be to avoid fatigue before going on a road trip as well as what your precautions will be during the trip to keep yourself awake and alert.

_____

_____

_____

_____

_____

_____

_____

Short-Term Physical Conditions and Driving

A. For each sentence below, circle T if the statement is true and F if it is false. If the statement is false, correct it in the space below.

1. You can drive after taking any medication prescribed by a doctor.   T   F

_____

2. Temporary injuries can make it risky for you to drive.   T   F

_____

3. Having the flu can affect the way you drive.   T   F

_____

4. It is always safe to drive after taking over-the-counter medications.   T   F

_____

5. The best defense against carbon monoxide poisoning is keeping your windows closed.   T   F

_____

B. If you must drive while you are ill or injured, list some ways in which you can compensate for your impaired condition.

_____

_____

_____

_____

C. FIND OUT MORE. What if you had a cold and had to go on a trip? What kind of medication could you safely use? To find out, go to a local drugstore and look at the packages of cold remedies that they sell. Make a list of the ones that do not cause drowsiness.

_____

_____

_____

_____

_____

STUDY GUIDE FOR CHAPTER 16   LESSON 3

Long-Term Physical Factors and Driving

A. Many people who are physically challenged can now drive motor vehicles with the aid of certain improvements that have been made in technology and science. Some physical challenges are listed below. In the space next to each physical challenge, describe what can be used to make it possible for the person to drive.

1. People without full use of their legs _____

2. People without arms _____

3. People who use wheelchairs _____

4. People who can't turn their heads or shoulders _____

B. For each sentence below, circle T if the statement is true and F if it is false. Correct each false statement in the space below.

1. A person with a spinal cord injury cannot get a license to drive.   T   F

_____

2. Another term for an *artificial limb* is *prosthetic device.*   T   F

_____

3. People between the ages of 50 and 75 have the highest pedestrian death rates.   T   F

_____

4. Anybody with a physical challenge can now get a driver's license.   T   F

_____

5. An older person generally has a slightly faster reaction time than a younger person.   T   F

_____

C. FIND OUT MORE. Call your state's Department of Motor Vehicles and ask them what the procedure is for a physically challenged person to get a driver's license in your state. How are the tests administered? For what length of time are the licenses issued?

_____

_____

_____

_____

_____

_____

CHAPTER 17 Psychological and Social Readiness

STUDY GUIDE FOR CHAPTER 17   LESSON 1

Inattention and Distraction

A. There are many sources of distractions for drivers that can make it unsafe to drive. How would you handle the following distractions?

Radio, cassette or CD player _____

_____

_____

Headphones _____

_____

_____

Cellular phones _____

_____

_____

Loud, rowdy passengers _____

_____

_____

Restless children _____

_____

_____

Animals in the vehicle _____

_____

_____

Toll roads _____

_____

_____

B. FIND OUT MORE. Call your local pet store. What devices are sold to keep dogs and cats restrained in vehicles?

_____

_____

STUDY GUIDE FOR CHAPTER 17   LESSON 2

Emotions

A. Strong emotions are a part of life. Being a good driver means knowing yourself well enough not to let your emotions interfere with your driving, and sometimes this means not driving at all. Indicate which of the guidelines below would be appropriate for each of the situations described. (Some situations can have more than one guideline.)

Guidelines

a. Identify situations that can lead to upsets.

b. Plan your trip to allow enough time.

c. Expect other drivers to make mistakes.

d. Delay driving when upset.

Situations

_____ **1.** The person you had been dating started going out with your best friend last week. You have been having a hard time sleeping and doing your homework.

_____ **2.** You just got your license and are getting ready to take your mother for a ride. Your mother tells you that she cannot pay for your car insurance as she had promised.

_____ **3.** It is Thanksgiving Day. You have to drive 100 miles in a snowstorm and arrive by noon.

_____ **4.** The vehicle in front of you stops short, and you brake with a jolt.

_____ **5.** You have a summer job delivering newspapers by car. Your boss and some of your customers often irritate you.

_____ **6.** The check you expected in the mail is not there. You owe your friend money, which you had promised you would pay back today. You feel panicky.

_____ **7.** You know that you are going to start a new job on Monday, and you are going away for the weekend.

_____ **8.** Construction has started on a bridge along your route. You dread the drive home.

_____ **9.** You are driving home after a basketball game in which you made a dumb play. You cannot stop thinking about the game.

_____ **10.** The vehicle in front of you drives very slowly up to a signal and then speeds up through the yellow light. You have to stop for the red light.

B. FIND OUT MORE. Interview five people who drive. What kinds of driving situations make them angry or upset? What makes them lose their concentration while driving?

_____

_____

_____

Norms and Peers

A. Match the term on the left with its definition on the right.

_____ **1.** negative peer pressure

_____ **2.** norm

_____ **3.** custom

_____ **4.** peer pressure

_____ **5.** laws

a. behaviors that satisfy people's needs for comfortably interacting with each other.

b. rules or standards of behavior that govern how people behave in different situations.

c. the influence of people who are in your age group.

d. the kind of influence that leads you to do something that you normally would not do.

e. rules that seek to fashion and regulate behavior by formal sanctions and official penalties.

B. For each sentence below, circle T if the statement is true and F if it is false. If the statement is false, correct it in the space below.

1. The potential for risky driving behavior increases in socially energized situations.   T   F

_____

2. As a driver, you are responsible for your own safety as well as that of your passengers.   T   F

_____

3. It is not necessary to pull over and park your vehicle if you have a serious or emotional matter to discuss with a companion.   T   F

_____

4. High-risk drivers habitually deviate from driving norms.   T   F

_____

5. Violating traffic laws can result in fines, imprisonment, vehicle impounding, and loss of license.   T   F

_____

C. FIND OUT MORE. Describe your strategy for dealing with negative peer pressure in a driving situation.

_____

_____

_____

_____

_____

CHAPTER 18   Handling Social Pressures

STUDY GUIDE FOR CHAPTER 18   LESSON 1

Alcohol and You

A. For each sentence below, circle T if the statement is true and F if it is false. Correct each false statement in the space below.

1. Peer pressure can influence the way you walk and talk.   T   F

_____

2. Alcohol is a powerful drug.   T   F

_____

3. There are ways to tell before you start drinking if it will eventually become a problem for you.   T   F

_____

4. Choosing not to drink guarantees that you will not become addicted to alcohol.   T   F

_____

5. Frequent lateness and absences from school are not a sign of problem drinking.   T   F

_____

6. People have no responsibility to protect themselves and others from the threat of people who drink and drive.   T   F

_____

7. A support group for young people who have an alcoholic friend, parent, or sibling is Alateen.   T   F

_____

8. Alcohol abuse can cause malnutrition.   T   F

_____

B. FIND OUT MORE. Go to your library. Look up any information that you can find on teenage alcoholism, and write what you find below.

_____

_____

_____

_____

Alcohol and Its Effects

A. Check the facts in the graph below and answer the questions. The graph is based on the effects of alcohol on a 150-pound adult male who has had four or more years of experience driving and who is an experienced drinker as well.

ELIMINATION RATE
Blood Alcohol Concentration (BAC)

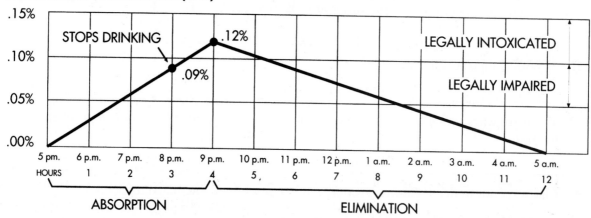

1. For how long does alcohol remain in a person's blood? _____

2. Between what hours should the person in the graph not drive? _____

3. For approximately how long is this person legally impaired? _____

4. Between what hours is the person legally intoxicated? _____

5. For how long after the person stops drinking is he legally impaired? _____

6. What is the alcohol level at the time elimination starts? _____

7. How long does it take for the alcohol to be eliminated? _____

8. Is the person legally impaired for a longer period while absorbing the alcohol or while

   eliminating the alcohol? _____

B. FIND OUT MORE. Search your local newspaper for one week. Keep a list of all accidents related to alcohol, and describe one of them below.

_____

_____

_____

_____

STUDY GUIDE FOR CHAPTER 18   LESSON 3

Other Drugs' Effect on Driving Ability

A. For each sentence below, circle T if the statement is true and F if it is false. Correct each false statement in the space below.

1. Over-the-counter drugs are drugs that you can purchase only with a prescription.   T   F

_____

2. Over-the-counter drugs will not interfere with your driving ability.   T   F

_____

3. A depressant slows down the central nervous system.   T   F

_____

4. Alcohol is a stimulant.   T   F

_____

5. Stimulants can make users think that they are more alert than usual.   T   F

_____

6. The chemicals in marijuana can stay in your body for as long as 6 hours.   T   F

_____

7. LSD is a kind of depressant.   T   F

_____

8. Marijuana can make the user feel drowsy.   T   F

_____

B. FIND OUT MORE. Collect your local newspaper for a week. Write a brief summary of any articles that you find about the problems associated with drugs and alcohol. Pay particular attention to what is happening in your community.

_____

_____

_____

_____

_____

_____

_____

STUDY GUIDE FOR CHAPTER 18   LESSON 4

Preventing Impaired Driving

A. In the space provided below, describe each legal measure for dealing with drivers who use alcohol or drugs.

Administrative License Revocation _____

_____

_____

_____

_____

Zero Tolerance Laws _____

_____

_____

_____

_____

Open Containers _____

_____

_____

_____

_____

Blood Alcohol Concentration _____

_____

_____

_____

_____

B. FIND OUT MORE. Which addiction support groups operate in your area? What services do these groups offer to the community? How might have these groups positively affected the roadway?

_____

_____

CHAPTER 19 Vehicle Readiness

STUDY GUIDE FOR CHAPTER 19   LESSON 1

Checking Your Vehicle

A. For each sentence below, circle T if the statement is true and F if it is false. Correct each false statement in the space below.

1. You should check the engine oil level only when the engine is running.   T   F

_____

2. The radiator cap should be opened only when the radiator is cool.   T   F

_____

3. A fan belt should be replaced every 5000 miles.   T   F

_____

4. Your vehicle's brake warning light will make you aware of any brake problems the vehicle may have.   T   F

_____

5. Brakes should be tested once a month.   T   F

_____

6. You should check your vehicle's headlights and turn signals every week.   T   F

_____

7. You can't know the specific guidelines for servicing your vehicle.   T   F

_____

8. You should ask a mechanic for an estimate before work begins on your vehicle.   T   F

_____

9. With newer vehicles, many repairs are covered under the vehicle's warranty.   T   F

_____

10. You should check your vehicle's battery cables to make sure that they are not too tight.   T   F

_____

B. FIND OUT MORE. Talk to a friend or relative who owns a vehicle. Ask if you can check the vehicle out as a part of your driver's training. Check the battery terminals, oil level, transmission fluid level, coolant level, hoses, wires, and fan belts. Let the owner know what you found, and write your findings below.

_____

_____

Maintaining Vehicle Systems

A. Match the following terms by placing the letter of the definition or the description of what the item does to the left of the item.

_____	**1.** coolant	**a.**	protects vehicle's electrical circuits from overloading
_____	**2.** exhaust manifold	**b.**	pumps coolant through radiator and engine
_____	**3.** muffler	**c.**	collects unburned gasses
_____	**4.** tailpipe	**d.**	another name for alternator
_____	**5.** catalytic converter	**e.**	mixture of water and antifreeze
_____	**6.** carbon monoxide	**f.**	key is used here to start vehicle
_____	**7.** battery	**g.**	supplies electricity needed to keep engine running
_____	**8.** ignition switch	**h.**	quiets engine noise
_____	**9.** alternator	**i.**	moves oil to all moving engine parts
_____	**10.** engine control module	**j.**	controls flow of coolant
_____	**11.** generator	**k.**	where exhaust gases exit vehicle
_____	**12.** fuse	**l.**	an odorless, deadly gas
_____	**13.** oil pump	**m.**	controls electric and other vehicle systems
_____	**14.** water pump	**n.**	reduces harmful gas emissions
_____	**15.** thermostat	**o.**	provides energy to start the engine

B. FIND OUT MORE. Go to your library and find out how a catalytic converter works. Describe your findings below. You may also make a diagram in the space below to show how the catalytic converter works.

_____

_____

_____

_____

_____

_____

_____

_____

_____

Suspension, Steering, Brakes, and Tires

A. For each sentence below, circle T if the statement is true and F if it is false. Correct each false statement in the space below.

   1. The main parts of a suspension system are the springs and the tires.   T   F

   _____

   2. Springs are designed to soften the impact of bumps in the roadway.   T   F

   _____

   3. Tire tread depth should be at least 1/26 inch.   T   F

   _____

   4. Your vehicle's tires should be rotated at least every 5000 to 6000 miles.   T   F

   _____

   5. There should be no more than two inches of play in the steering wheel if your vehicle has power steering.   T   F

   _____

B. There are several clues that a vehicle's front end is out of alignment or that the tires need balancing. What are they?

   _____

   _____

C. FIND OUT MORE. Ask somebody you know who has a vehicle if you may inspect their tires. What did you check for, and what did you find?

   _____

   _____

   _____

   _____

   _____

   _____

   _____

   _____

Child Safety Seats

A. For each sentence below, circle T if the statement is true and F if it is false. Correct each false statement in the space below.

1. When traveling in a vehicle, children of all ages should wear a safety belt.   T   F

_____

2. All 50 states require that children under the age of four be secured in child safety seats.   T   F

_____

3. Rear-facing child safety seats are designed for infants who weigh less than 20 pounds.   T   F

_____

4. A rear-facing child safety seat should be placed in front of an airbag for added security.   T   F

_____

5. A convertible child safety seat is designed for infants who weigh more than 20 pounds.   T   F

_____

6. Children over one year old and weighing more than 20 pounds should ride in a forward-facing child safety seat.   T   F

_____

7. Booster seats position younger children so that seat belts fit correctly.   T   F

_____

8. A lap belt should be positioned across a child's stomach.   T   F

_____

9. Children are safest in the front seat of a vehicle.   T   F

_____

10. An adult seat belt will not properly fit children until they are at least 4'9" and weigh about 80 pounds.   T   F

_____

B. FIND OUT MORE. Go to your state's DMV Web site or your local library. Look up any information that you can find on injury prevention and child safety seats. Write what you find below.

_____

_____

_____

Skill Review for New Drivers: *Alcohol and the Driver*

Under the Influence

Be aware of signs that other drivers on the road may be under the influence of alcohol or other drugs. Various signs indicate possible problems.

Traveling at erratic speeds-either too fast or too slow Alcohol-impaired drivers often have trouble driving at a steady speed.

Running over curbs or turning into the wrong lane Alcohol-impaired drivers are often unable to turn smoothly.

Weaving from side to side Alcohol-impaired drivers suffer from loss of coordination, which affects their ability to steer smoothly.

Ignoring or overshooting traffic signs Alcohol-impaired drivers suffer impaired reflexes and vision loss.

If you find yourself on the same roadway as a driver who shows any of these signs, increase the amount of space between your vehicles. Be alert to the fact that there is an impaired driver sharing the roadway with you. If possible, inform a police officer of what you have noticed.

Ten misconceptions about drinking.

1. **All drinks are equal in alcohol content.**

   FACT: This is only true sometimes. For instance, coolers are popular alcoholic drinks for some young people. A cooler may have 50 percent more alcohol content than a 1-ounce shot of whiskey. When a 12-ounce can or bottle of regular beer is compared to a 1-ounce shot of 80-proof whiskey ($\frac{1}{2}$ of the proof = alcohol percentage), the beer actually has 35 percent more alcohol. This is important for two reasons:

   For a person drinking beer, the more a person drinks, the wider the gap becomes.

   About 80 percent of persons charged with DWI or DUI were drinking beer prior to their arrest.

   The most important concept to remember is that both the size of the drink (ounces) and strength of the drink (percentage of alcohol) have to be known before any meaningful comparison can be made. No matter how big the glass, more alcohol means a stronger drink, with stronger effects.

2. **The human body removes one drink per hour.**

   FACT: This is only true for some people. Alcohol does eventually pass out of your body, but it is a dangerous concept that the human body can always remove one drink per hour. Even if standard drink sizes are used, this removal rate is true only for very obese or very large people. The truth is that the average elimination rate is .015 percent per hour.

3. **Males and females handle alcohol the same.**

   FACT: Not true. It is harder for females to handle alcohol because females have much less of an enzyme called alcohol dehydrogenase in their stomach than males. Since this enzyme breaks down alcohol, females absorb more alcohol into their bloodstream than males do. Females also tend to have more body fat than males, another factor in blood alcohol concentration.

4. **Beer is not as intoxicating as hard liquor.**

   FACT: Not true. While there is more alcohol in an ounce of liquor than in an ounce of beer, beer contains enough alcohol to intoxicate you.

5. **You cannot get drunk on a full stomach.**

   FACT: A full stomach does mean the alcohol is absorbed into the bloodstream a little more slowly. However, all of that alcohol will still get into the bloodstream and travel to the brain and other parts of the body.

6. **Impaired (drinking) driving is not dangerous.**

   FACT: Not true. Motor-vehicle crashes are the number-one killer of teens. Motor-vehicle crashes kill more 16- to 20-year-olds each year than homicide, suicide, cancer, accidental poisoning, and heart disease combined.

7. **You must drink because your friends want you to, even if you are the driver.**

   FACT: Real friends would not want you to hurt yourself or others. Resist peer pressure in this dangerous situation. Tell your friends the facts about alcohol.

8. **Black coffee, a cold shower, lots of exercise, or all three together can quickly sober up a drinker.**

   FACT: Not true. The body cannot burn much more than ½–ounce of alcohol in an hour. Nothing can really speed up the process.

9. **Alcohol makes you feel better when you are depressed.**

   FACT: Alcohol is a depressant, or "downer." Even if it lifts you up for a minute, it may leave you feeling worse than before.

10. **Sometimes, because of peer pressure at a party, there is no other choice but to drink.**

    FACT: You do have a choice. You do not have to drink alcohol—you can drink something else. Abstinence is the only responsible action for anyone under age 21.

Skill Review for New Drivers: *The In-Vehicle Test*

Practicing for the In-Vehicle Test

When practicing your driving, here are some of the skills you may need to demonstrate. You will learn about these skills in Chapters 5, 6, and 8.

- parallel parking
- starting and stopping smoothly
- shifting gears
- backing up safely
- turning
- passing
- following at a safe distance
- signaling
- executing turnabouts

Choosing a Vehicle for the Test

Suppose you have practiced in and are equally comfortable driving two vehicles, both of which are in good mechanical condition. Which vehicle should you choose to use for your in-vehicle test? Here are some tips that may make your decision easier.

- Choose a vehicle with an automatic transmission over one with a manual transmission. Nervousness can make you have trouble coordinating the clutch, the gearshift, and the accelerator.
- Choose a smaller vehicle over a larger one. Smaller vehicles are generally easier to maneuver.
- Choose a conservative, family-type vehicle over a sports car or "souped-up" vehicle. Make a good first impression on the examiner.

Skill Review for New Drivers: *Be Prepared*

Emergency Items

Keep emergency items in the trunk of your vehicle. Include such items as these:

- flashlight with extra batteries
- jumper cables (for starting a dead battery)
- flares, warning triangles, or reflectors
- coolant
- windshield-washer fluid
- wiping cloth
- ice scraper, snow brush, and snow shovel.
- jack with flat board for soft surfaces
- lug wrench (for changing a flat tire)
- screwdriver, pliers, duct tape, and adjustable wrench for making simple repairs

- extra fan/alternator belt
- extra fuses (if needed for your vehicle)
- fire extinguisher
- heavy gloves
- blanket
- drinking water
- first aid kit
- pencil and notebook (for recording emergency information)
- spare head lamp and bulb

Stuck in the Snow?

If you get stuck in snow, you may be able to free your vehicle by "rocking" it. Follow the steps below.

1. Keep your front wheels pointed straight ahead, if possible. The vehicle will move more easily in a straight line.
2. Shift back and forth between Drive (or First gear) and Reverse. Accelerate forward slowly and steadily. When the vehicle will move forward no farther, press firmly on the brake to stop and hold the vehicle while you quickly shift to Reverse.
3. Release the brake and accelerate with gentle pressure as far back as the vehicle will go until the wheels start to spin. Step on the brake again and hold it while shifting to Drive or First gear.
4. Repeat as necessary. Do not spin your wheels. You will only dig yourself in.

Repeat these shifts as quickly and smoothly as possible, but be sure to use the brake to hold the vehicle at a stop while you shift gears. Each forward-and-backward movement should take the vehicle a little farther in one direction or the other.

When rocking a vehicle, proceed cautiously. If the tires do suddenly grip, the vehicle may lurch forward, backward, or sideways. Warn bystanders to keep their distance, and take care not to strike nearby vehicles or objects.

Working a Self-Service Gas Pump

To operate a self-service gas pump, pull up to the pump that dispenses the kind of fuel your vehicle uses. If a sign says "Pay Cashier Before Pumping," the pumps will not operate until you pay. Otherwise, pump the amount you need, and pay when you are done.

1. Open the fuel filler door and take off the gas cap.
2. Take the pump nozzle off its cradle, and place it in the fuel tank opening.
3. Turn on the pump switch. It is usually located near the pump nozzle cradle.
4. Squeeze the lever on the pump nozzle to begin pumping the fuel.
5. If you have paid in advance, or when the tank is full, the pump will shut off automatically. If you did not prepay, release the nozzle lever, turn off the pump switch, and put the nozzle back in its cradle. Then put the gas cap back on, and shut the fuel filler door.

Skill Review for New Drivers: *Driving Behavior*

Being Pulled Over

What should you do if you are pulled over by the police?

- Stay calm.
- Remain in your vehicle, keeping your hands visible.
- Produce requested documents quickly and efficiently.
- Be courteous. Do not argue with, insult, or touch the officer.
- Do not lie, cry, or make excuses.
- Never try to bribe the officer. Bribery is illegal!

Managing Time

Effective time management begins before you get behind the wheel. Here are some tips.

- Make a conscious effort to understand and learn to judge time and speed factors. Try to develop a sense, for example, of how much longer it takes a vehicle to slow down and stop when moving at 50 mph than at 20 mph.
- Plan your route in advance, and always allow yourself plenty of time to reach your destination.
- Get traffic information from the radio or other source to help you plan the best route of travel.

Fighting Fatigue

Fatigue is usually temporary and easily overcome. The best way to overcome fatigue is to stop doing whatever you're doing and get some rest.

Before You Drive

- Get plenty of rest.
- Avoid heavy, fatty foods.
- Don't drink alcoholic beverages.

While You Drive

Make sure there is a good flow of fresh air in the vehicle. If your vehicle is overheated or poorly ventilated, you may become sleepy.

- Wear sunglasses to cope with glare from sun and snow.
- Take turns driving with someone else.
- Turn on the radio. Sing, whistle, or talk to yourself.
- Stop regularly, get out of the vehicle, and walk, jog, or do other light exercise for a few minutes.

Problem Behavior

When you search the roadway, observe the behavior of other drivers for clues to potential problems. Watch for drivers:

- taking their eyes off the road while talking with others.
- using cellular phones.
- smoking, eating, reading, or looking at a map.
- with unusual postures at the wheel, which may indicate intoxication.
- signaling late or not at all.
- moving too slowly or too rapidly or following too closely (tailgating).
- drifting from side to side in their lane.
- whose view may be obstructed by packages, objects, or tall passengers.
- with out-of-state license plates, who may be searching for an address or may be unaccustomed to driving in your area.

Skill Review for New Drivers: *Driving Maneuvers*

Holding the Vehicle in Place

Learning to move a manual-shift vehicle forward after stopping on an uphill grade takes practice. To keep the vehicle from rolling backward, follow these steps.

1. Set the parking brake.
2. Press the clutch to the floor, and shift into First gear.
3. Let the clutch pedal up to the friction point, and press gently on the accelerator.
4. Release the parking brake as you begin to feel the vehicle pulling forward.
5. Press the accelerator as you let up the clutch pedal.
6. Accelerate in First gear until you have gained enough speed to shift into Second gear.

Do not hold your vehicle in place on a hill by pressing the gas pedal slightly while keeping the clutch near the friction point. "Riding the clutch" this way wears your clutch needlessly. Always brake to keep your vehicle from rolling back.

Accelerating

- For best control when accelerating, rest your heel on the floor, and press the pedal gently with your toes.
- As a general rule, accelerate gradually. Beginning drivers sometimes make errors when they increase speed quickly. Accelerating gradually also saves fuel.
- No two vehicles accelerate exactly the same way. When driving an unfamiliar vehicle, allow yourself time to get used to the feel of the gas pedal and to the vehicle's acceleration capability.

Drying the Brakes

Wet brakes do not work as efficiently as dry brakes. After you have driven through heavy rain or deep puddles, check for wet brakes. If you apply the brakes lightly and the vehicle pulls to one side or does not slow, your brakes are probably wet. Dry the brakes by driving slowly; apply light pressure on the brake pedal. The friction created will generate heat, which will dry the brakes.

Skill Review for New Drivers: *Interacting on the Roadway*

Communicating with Other Drivers

Your safety, the safety of your passengers, and the safety of other roadway users depend to a large extent on how well you communicate, with other drivers and with pedestrians. Good roadway communication involves giving clear signals and warnings, paying attention to signals and warnings given by other drivers, and noticing where pedestrians are and what they are doing.

Drivers exchange four basic kinds of communication.

Intentions   plan to turn left or right; slowing down; plan to pass (please move over); plan to back up

Warnings   trouble ahead in my lane; need to stop suddenly; danger in your lane; headlights are blinding

Presence   parked vehicle, disabled vehicle

Feedback   recognizing another driver's signal; recognizing the presence of a pedestrian; thanks to a driver for allowing you to pass

Here is how to communicate.

Electronic signals   turn-signal lights, brake lights, backup lights, emergency hazard flashers; horn (short, sharp, or steady blasts); headlights (flash on and off, switch from high to low beams)

Body gestures   hand signals; nodding up and down; shaking head sideways; smiling; puzzled or confused look; raised eyebrows

Identifying Information

Here are some objects and conditions to identify as you drive:

- vehicles, pedestrians, or objects that are in your path or could enter your path
- vehicles, pedestrians, or objects close to the back or sides of your vehicle
- vehicles, objects, or roadway features that limit your visibility and may conceal objects or conditions
- signs, signals, and roadway markings
- roadway surface conditions

How to Safely Share the Roadway with a Truck

- Always allow at least a 4-second following distance to make yourself visible to the truck and to allow you to see more of the roadway.
- When stopping behind a truck stopped at a sign or signal, allow extra distance in case the truck rolls back when starting.
- Allow yourself extra time and space when passing. When a large truck is about to pass you, steer to compensate for the gust of air caused by the truck.
- If a truck is bearing down on you as you drive downhill, move into another lane or pullover to let the truck pass.
- Try not to drive on the right side of a truck, especially just below the right-front passenger side. This is a blind spot for the truck driver.
- Never try to drive by the right side of a truck at an intersection if the truck's right-hand signal is on, even if the truck is in the left lane.
- Large trucks make very wide right-hand turns.
- Never pass a truck on the right side of the roadway.
- After passing a truck, do not pull right in front of it after you clear it. Leave plenty of room in case you have to apply your brakes.

Skill Review for New Drivers: *Night Driving*

Driving at Night

When you drive at night, you need to compensate for reduced visibility. Here are some steps to take:

- Drive more slowly than you would during the day. Adjust your speed to the range of your headlights. Increase your following distance to 3 or 4 seconds or more.
- Keep your eyes moving. Do not stare at brightly lit areas. Keep your attention on the street-level activities around you and in the direction in which you are heading.
- Make sure your windshield and headlights are clean.
- Use your headlights wisely. Use your high beams when possible, such as on long stretches of empty highway. Switch to low beams for city driving and when following vehicles or meeting oncoming vehicles.
- Avoid driving near your usual bedtime. Your level of alertness is low at this time.

More Suggestions for Dealing with Visibility Problems at Night

- Slow down. Remember that your visibility is limited.
- Avoid looking directly into the headlights of oncoming vehicles.
- When necessary to maintain your bearings, glance down at the right edge of your traffic lane beyond oncoming vehicles.
- To remind an approaching driver that his or her high beams are on, quickly switch your own headlights from low to high and back again.
- If you can adjust your rearview mirror for night driving, do so to cut glare from the headlights of vehicles behind you.
- If you must stop along the road, use your emergency flashers to enable other drivers to see you.
- Watch for animals, joggers, bicyclists, and obstacles on the road.
- Always remove sunglasses once the sun sets.

Skill Review for New Drivers: *Think Before You Act*

Don't Rush Yourself

If your state has not implemented a graduated driver licensing system, you might want to consider creating a plan of your own based on the GDL recommendations in the lesson. For several months after you have received your license, continue to practice driving only with a licensed adult in the vehicle. Then drive unsupervised for another

50 hours, limiting your driving to the hours between 5 A.M. and midnight. Remember that when you are behind the wheel, you have assumed responsibility for yourself and for others. Take that responsibility seriously: Lives depend on it.

Used Vehicle Checks

When purchasing a used vehicle, check the following:

The condition of the paint   New paint can indicate collision damage.

For rust   Do not buy a vehicle with rusted-out areas unless you can afford repairs.

For worn tires, including the spare   Uneven wear on any tire may indicate front-end problems.

The tailpipe   A light-gray color indicates proper combustion.

The radiator   Remove the radiator cap. Is the coolant clean? Is there caked-on rust on the cap? Are there signs of leaks on the back of the radiator?

The transmission   Pullout the transmission dipstick and sniff it. A burnt smell may indicate an overheated transmission. Feel the oil on the crankcase dipstick. If it is gritty, there may be dirt in the engine.

The service stickers   Service stickers tell you how often a vehicle has been tuned and had the oil changed.

All windows and door locks   Check for ease of operation.

The engine   Listen for loud or unusual noises when you start the vehicle. Check all gauges and warning lights.

For slamming sounds or lurching as the vehicle starts   An automatic transmission should take hold promptly when in gear.

Skill Review for New Drivers: *Vehicle Care*

15-Minute Checkup

To keep your vehicle in good working order, follow the suggestions in your owner's manual for periodic checkups and maintenance. In addition, if you drive 10,000 or more miles a year, do a 15-minute checkup every month.

- all lights for burned-out bulbs
- the battery fluid level or, if your vehicle has a sealed battery, the green battery-charge indicator
- the engine oil level and transmission fluid level
- the brake pedal for firmness and proper operation
- the brake fluid level
- the air pressure in all tires
- the tires for uneven wear
- the cooling system
- the hoses and belts that operate the fan and the compressor
- the windshield washer and wipers
- the power steering fluid level

Having Your Vehicle Serviced or Repaired

- To find a reliable mechanic or garage, ask friends and relatives for their recommendations. You can also call your local AAA.
- Ask the mechanic for a cost estimate of the work to be done.
- Find out for how long the mechanic will guarantee any work done. Save your bill or receipt.
- Know what you're paying for. If there is something you don't understand, ask for an explanation.
- If the mechanic replaces a part, ask to see the old part.
- Warranties may cover many repairs. Know what your warranty does and does not cover.

Skill Review for New Drivers: *Safety First*

Shared Left-Turn Lanes

Here are tips for using shared left-turn lanes safely:

- Do not get in the lane too soon. The longer you stay in the lane, the more likely it is you will meet someone coming in the opposite direction.
- Watch for vehicles pulling out of entrances and side streets. They may cross in front of you, cutting you off.
- Don't use a shared left-turn lane for anything but turning left.

Parking Beyond an Intersection

Be especially careful if you have decided to park in a space or make a turn just beyond an intersection. Follow these steps:

1. Do not signal right or left as you approach the intersection. Other drivers may think you are going to turn at the intersection.
2. If other vehicles are near the intersection, move carefully into the correct lane and slow down.
3. Use your signals only after you have entered the intersection.

Leaving a Vehicle Safely

Do not be careless. Learn the safe way to leave your vehicle.

- With your foot firmly on the brake pedal, set the parking brake.
- Shift into Park (automatic) or Reverse (manual).
- Close all windows.
- Turn the key to the lock position, and remove it from the ignition switch. Turn your steering wheel slightly to lock it too.
- Check for approaching traffic. Look in your mirrors and check your blind spot.
- Wait for a break in traffic before opening the door. Then open it only far enough and long enough to get out of the vehicle.
- Lock the door. Then, keeping an eye on traffic, move quickly around the rear of the vehicle toward the curb.
- Whenever possible, have passengers exit from the curb side of the vehicle.

Pedestrians to Watch For

Certain pedestrians require drivers to pay special attention.

- Elderly pedestrians may have impaired eyesight or hearing. They may move and react slowly and require extra time to cross streets.
- People with physical challenges, such as people who are blind and people in wheelchairs, may need extra time to cross streets.
- Pedestrians with strollers or carriages may need extra time to move onto or off of a sidewalk.
- Joggers running with their backs to traffic can pose a hazard. Many do not wear reflective clothing, which makes them difficult to see when visibility is low.
- People on the job, such as mail carriers, delivery people, or roadway maintenance workers, may be distracted by their work and step out into the roadway without checking traffic.
- Umbrellas and hooded parkas may impair pedestrians' ability to notice traffic.

Notes

Notes

Notes